A GRAFFITI GUIDE TO SEX IN
OUR TIMES

GRAFFITI 5

AS THE ACTRESS
SAID TO THE BISHOP

KILROY & McLACHLAN

Also by Roger Kilroy & Edward McLachlan

GRAFFITI I: THE SCRAWL OF THE WILD
GRAFFITI II: THE WALLS OF THE WORLD
GRAFFITI III: THE GOLDEN GRAFFITI AWARDS
GRAFFITI IV: THE EMPIRE WRITES BACK
ILLUMINATED LIMERICKS
KISS ME, HARDY

and published by Corgi Books

A GRAFFITI GUIDE TO SEX IN OUR TIMES

GRAFFITI 5

AS THE ACTRESS SAID TO THE BISHOP

KILROY & McLACHLAN

For lovers of religion & good taste.

GRAFFITI 5: AS THE ACTRESS SAID TO THE BISHOP
A CORGI BOOK 0 552 99045 0

First publication in Great Britain

PRINTING HISTORY

Corgi edition published 1983

Corgi Books are published by Transworld Publishers Ltd.,
Century House, 61-63 Uxbridge Road, Ealing, London W5 5SA

Made and printed in Great Britain by the Guernsey Press Co. Ltd.,
Guernsey, Channel Islands.

CONTENTS

When you've Adam, don't they make you Eve?

EVE WAS THE FIRST FEMINIST — SHE TRIED TO BRING ABOUT THE FALL OF MAN.

Adam 'ad 'em!

I love turning over new leaves, with my snake.

Why is it that women use sex to get love, and men use love to get sex.

Before you meet your handsome prince — you have to kiss an awful lot of toads

ORAL SEX IS A MATTER OF TASTE

CHASTITY IS ITS OWN PUNISHMENT

How do girls get minks?
— The same way minks
get minks.

IF SEX IS A PAIN IN THE ARSE,
YOU'RE DOING IT WRONG.

Seduction is the art of
genital persuasion.

What goes in dry, comes out wet and gives warm satisfaction — A teabag.

YOU'RE NEVER ALONE IF YOU'RE A SEX MANIAC.

Some things are better left unshed

MY BODY IS AN OUTLAW — IT'S WANTED ALL OVER TOWN

Is a book on voyeurism called a Peeping Tome?

The latest sex manual is all embracing.

MAKE LOVE NOT WAR — IT'S CHEAPER

No sex without participation.

I'M ON PIECE WORK
— AND THE PIECE I'M
WORKING ON IS GLORIA

The word for today is 'legs':
— Spread the word!

LOVE MAKES THE WORLD GO DOWN

Sex kills
— die happy

If there are plenty more pebbles on the beach, why haven't I had a shingle offer.

LOVE WILL GET YOU THROUGH TIMES OF NO SEX BETTER THAN SEX WILL GET YOU THROUGH TIMES OF NO LOVE

MY HEART AND I CALL TO YOU..... BUT YOU'RE TOO DEAF TO EROS.

18

PUPPY LOVE
ALWAYS
GOES TO THE
DOGS

If at first
you don't succeed.....

which of us is the opposite sex?

SEX IS ALL RIGHT BUT
IT'S NOT AS GOOD AS
THE REAL THING.

Courtship is when you
try each other for sighs.

Disco Dancing
is for jerks.

ASK ME
-I MIGHT.

Cuddle,
don't quarrel.

IT PAYS TO ADVERTISE

FROG needs beautiful princess to break spell. Box 169.

SUGAR DADDY urgently seeks enormously plump jelly baby. Box 101.

MILLIONAIRE needed for correspondence. Genuine Box 164.

GLASGOW male wishes to worship large breasts. Send details to Box 138.

TIN MAN, 35, seeks girl or woman with oil-can. Box OZ 14.

APOLLO seeks Venus! Box 29.

GOODBYE GRETEL! Hansel seeks witch for satisfyingly wicked relationship. Box 176.

WANTED — Girl for breeding. Box M4.

Failed Woody Allen seeks failed Diane Keaton.
TELEPHONE 26395

Very ugly 80 year-old dwarf, seeks pretty girl, 17-23. This description of myself is not <u>entirely</u> accurately.
RING - 69241

Elderly pessimist seeks alcoholic sex kitten with view to marriage or similar. Ring 409728

OLD BORE SEEKS SIMILAR. EITHER SEX CONSIDERED IF DULL ENOUGH Call 881-9072

Like a nice time, dearie? RING 16238

Is free love free? Is it love? Let's help each other find out TEL — 074695

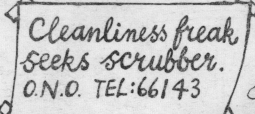

Cleanliness freak seeks scrubber. O.N.O. TEL: 66143

Girls! Are you looking for a brilliant young company director with a pad in New York, with a yacht in the Bahamas and a house in the country?
If so, fine. If not, write to me. I'm 38, well meaning and live in Muswell Hill.

IF YOU LIKE YOUR WINE LIKE YOUR WOMEN, INTOXICATING AND MATURE, CALL ROSE ON 771-842!
She's 80 and plastered!

Have a dirty weekend – explore an old coalmine

I used to think Fellatio was a character in Hamlet until I discovered Smirnoff.

DON'T DRINK AND DRIVE – YOU'LL ONLY SPILL IT.

Keep Britain green
- HAVE SEX WITH A FROG
Sank 'eaven for leetle gairls

FIRE EXIT

Yes, fire all supporters of euthanasia!

A MAN WRAPPED UP IN HIMSELF MAKES A VERY SMALL PARCEL.

NO SMOKING IN BED

AND NO SLEEPING IN ASHTRAYS

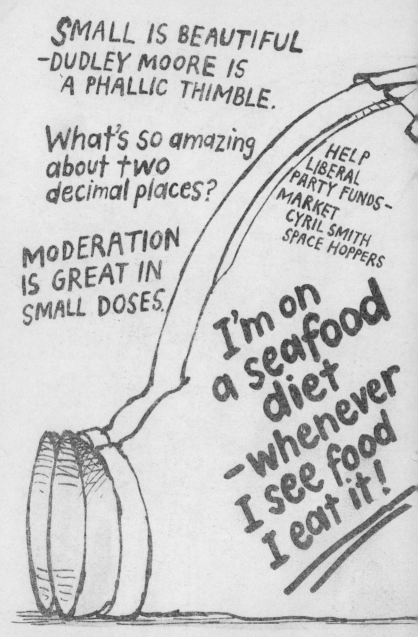

SMALL IS BEAUTIFUL
-DUDLEY MOORE IS
A PHALLIC THIMBLE.

What's so amazing
about two
decimal places?

MODERATION
IS GREAT IN
SMALL DOSES.

HELP
LIBERAL
PARTY FUNDS-
MARKET
CYRIL SMITH
SPACE HOPPERS

I'm on
a seafood
diet
-whenever
I see food
I eat it!

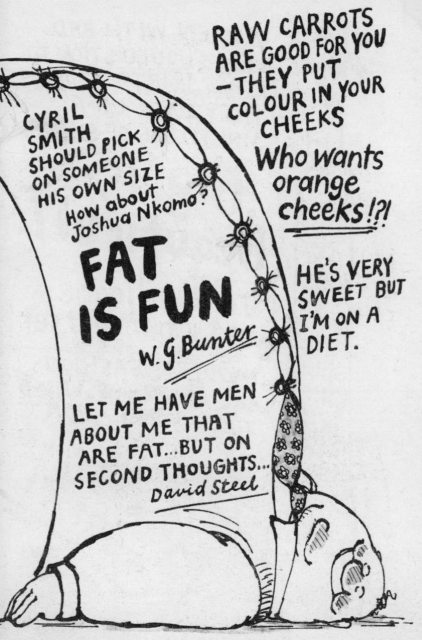

33

WOMEN WITH BAD LEGS SHOULD STICK TO LONG SKIRTS BECAUSE THEY COVER UP A MULTITUDE OF SHINS.

Big is beautiful!

Take silicone and join the jut set.

MODERN FASHIONS ARE OFTEN PRESENTED TONGUE IN CHIC!

A HOME-MADE DRESS LOOKS SEW-SEW.

The ends justify the jeans.

SHE MADE IT TO THE TOP BECAUSE HER CLOTHES DIDN'T

Janet Reger
—you were
wonderful!!

GRIN —AND BARE IT!

THE NOLANS ARE THE TOPS — DESPITE THE KNOCKERS

SEX APPEAL — GIVE GENEROUSLY

Be your sylph — practice girth control.

I'm in the punk of condition

YOU'RE JUST WHAT THE DOCTOR ORDERED — A PILL!

WHISTLE WHILE YOU LURK

Life is a bed of ruses

I'm suffering from Alice
— WHAT'S THAT?
I don't know,
but Christopher
Robin went
down with it!

DOCTOR'S ORDERS

WARD 7

Other vice may be nice but sex won't rot your teeth!

Jogging is good for the heart

SO IS KISSING AND CUDDLY

MUGGING IS GOOD FOR THE POCKET

—A.MUGGE

44

Little is known about the salivary glands because they are so secretive

If you ever had elephantiasis you'll never forget it!

The bride may not be
worth the expense
of the wedding;
Try her first.

I'M UN-ALTARABLE

THE ORGANIST WAS INSTRUMENTAL IN OUR MARRIAGE

Much 'I do' about nothing.

WHAT GOD HAS PUT ASUNDER
LET NO MAN JOIN TOGETHER.

A submissive
wife is a toy
forever.

Marriage is
    bliss parsonified.

PRIESTS CAN'T MARRY
WITHOUT PRIOR APPROVAL.

I'm footloose
and fiancée free.

Lead me to
    the halter, Walter.

Marriage is a bed of roses — Look out for the thorns.

IF THE BLONDE YOU MARRY TURNS OUT TO BE JUST A BRUNETTE, SUE HER FOR BLEACH OF PROMISE

Oh, how we danced on the night we were wed;
We danced and we danced
'cause the room had no bed!

Marriage is a lottery!

YES, BUT YOU CAN'T TEAR UP YOUR TICKET IF YOU LOSE!

MY WIFE'S CALLED PETAL.

Mine's called Flour
—She's been through the mill.

MAY ALL YOUR UPS & DOWNS BE IN THE BED.

MARRIAGE CAN DAMAGE YOUR HEALTH
Love and marriage go together like a horse and carnage.
...AND THEY LIVED HAPPILY EVER AFTER SOMEONE ELSE.
Give peace a
VIOLENCE SOARS
Wife clubs husband
Man shoots wife
Wife stabs husband
Husband strangles wife

EVER FAITHFUL

MONOGAMY LEAVES A LOT TO BE DESIRED

Not so much adultery as a lay of wife.

54

Give him enough rope – and he'll skip.

BIGAMIST IS AN ITALIAN FOG

His two-timing is perfect

HOW COME YOU NEVER TELL
ME WHEN YOU'RE HAVING
AN ORGASM?
Because you're never around!

Better to have loved
and lost than to have spent
your whole damn life with him.

THE ETERNAL TRIANGLE IS USUALLY RIGHT-ANGLED

ALL'S WELL THATS ENDS WELL

When all that's stiff
is his socks—
Take the money & run!

Spice is nicer than spouse.

JUST
DIVORCED

GJU 494

ONE MAN'S SUNDAY LUNCH
IS ONE WOMAN'S SUNDAY GONE!

A woman who thinks
the way to a man's heart
is through his stomach
is aiming a little too high.

OUR MARRIAGE IS
ALL PREACHES & SCREAM.

Your dinner's
in the cat!

59

An Englishman's home is his castle —so let him clean it!

AN EMPLOYED WIFE GETS TWO JOBS FOR THE PRICE OF ONE.

A wife is her husband's bitter half.

I'M GLAD THAT I'M A WOMAN, I'M GLAD THAT I AM FREE: BUT I WISH I WERE A LITTLE DOG AND MY HUSBAND WAS A TREE.

The crank in the driving seat happens to be my wife.

MY CAR HAS WIFE-ASSISTED STEERING

My wife took a crash course in driving!

My wife's driving me to drink!

My wife ran over.....   OUT

WARNING: MY WIFE LIKES TO PUT HER FOOT DOWN.

If your wife wants to learn to drive — Don't stand in her way!

hath no fury like a woman at the wheel.

Thank God, the upholstery's brown!!

IN A CAR, MY WIFE RUNNETH OVER

578   the Beast of Exmoor

63

LET SLEEPING GODS LIE.

She's my altered ego

I DON'T ARGUE WITH MY WIFE, IF I DO, WORDS FLAIL ME.

Don't wake up Grumpy —Let her lie in!

It costs nothing to
have a baby at Butlins.

IS A PAS DE DEUX
THE FATHER OF TWINS?

I'm zinc, therefore I'm a pram

Bad spellers of the world —untie!

Mummy, Mummy,
what's an orgasm?
I don't know, dear,
ask your father.

4 KIDS OR MORE AND YOU'RE
OVERBEARING.

Insanity is hereditary — you get it from your kids

"It's a hellova life!"
Said the Queen of Spain,
"Five months pleasure
    and nine month's pain;
Four weeks rest,
    and at it again,
It's a hellova life!"
    Said the Queen of Spain.

Every mother is a working mother

Men do not possess egos; They are possessed by them.

WOMEN WHO WANT TO BE EQUAL TO MEN LACK AMBITION

Show me a man who smiles at defeat and I'll show you a happy chiropodist.

MEN? HE! HE!

IF YOU WANT A CHICK — GO BUY AN EGG

A woman who calls herself a bird deserves to catch a lot of worms.

Make a snow-woman this winter

I was born a woman — I won't be told how to become one!

THE WALTZ WAS INVENTED BY MEN — FOR THEM TO LEAD AND STEP ON THE WOMAN AT THE SAME TIME.

What would the world be without men?
FREE OF CRIME AND FULL OF FAT, HAPPY WOMEN!
Dish it out – Don't cook it.
It's a man's world and the end is nigh!

Sex with men is a load of old balls

FREE WOMEN!
— Where?

CAN YOU BEAT MY TOTAL OF 71 MEN?
Yes-if you can supply the whips!

Women! Get out from under!

More female train drivers!
a woman's right to choo-choose.

A hard man is good to find!

He might have hairs
on his chest...
But, sister,
so does Lassie!

I REQUIRE ONLY THREE
THINGS OF A MAN—
HE MUST BE HANDSOME,
RUTHLESS & STUPID

A MAN WHO CALLS A WOMAN A BROAD IS NARROW.

ROSES ARE RED
VIOLETS ARE BLUE
AND MINE ARE WHITE.

Bottom pinchers are a pain in the arse

Vibrators are cheap
   and longer lasting.
They are always ready
   and never demanding
They never want to know
   if you have come or
Call you frigid
   if you don't and they
Don't make you pregnant,
   give you V.D. or snore.

WHEN A GIRL IS BIG ENOUGH, SHE'S OLD ENOUGH!

'AVE MARIA!
I don't mind if I do!

REMEMBER! EVEN THE MOST BEAUTIFUL WOMAN IN THE ROOM HAS PIMPLES ON HER BOTTOM.

A PURITAN IS A MAN
WHO NOES WHAT HE LIKES.

Give me an inch and
I'll take the whole 36-24-36

LIFE, LIBERTY AND THE HAPPINESS OF PURSUIT.

Small is beautiful?

All big women
die young
—That's why
we're left with
little old ladies.

There's a shortage of girls around here. I DON'T CARE HOW SHORT THEY ARE, THERE JUST AREN'T ENOUGH OF THEM!

Men who put women on pedestals rarely knock them off.

I've put my money into a new girlie magazine so I can take accrued interest.

GENERALLY SPEAKING WOMEN ARE

Put Womens libbers behind bras.

INSIDE EVERY GREAT CANNIBAL IS A WOMAN.

Richard II was a queen

BUT MARTIN LUTHER WAS A KING!

I LOVE QUEEN OF PUDDINGS.

I love fat faggots too!

EVERY GAY PERSON IS THE PRODUCT OF A HETEROSEXUAL RELATIONSHIP

Puff the magic drag one

I'm in love with a dozen soldiers — It's all very platoonic.

Why is that girl trying to pick up my girlfriend?

...and why is she carrying her off?

BE MISERABLE — GO GAY!

Are you a practising lesbian?

NO, THIS IS ABOUT AS GOOD AS I GET.

No wonder I'm confused — one of my parents was a woman and so was the other!

I'M EVERY OTHER INCH A GENTLEMAN

Bisexual man, aged 30 —seeks young married couple.

BOYS DON'T MAKE PASSES AT GIRLS WHO LOVE LASSES

I'm ready for sex of one kind.
— and half a dozen of the other!

HAVE A FAG — King-sized?
NO, BUT FILTER TIPPED.

Bisexuals never know whether they're coming or going.

PUT SOME FUN BETWEEN
YOUR LEGS —
BUY A MOTORBIKE.

MY car was built by robots
— but I'm very human...
and you should see my clutch!

THIS CAR IS FEMALE
— IT'S VERY RELIABLE
BUT DIFFICULT TO MOVE

clunk-Click. every trip
INVEST IN A CHASTITY BELT!

Is a lorry carrying live poultry flexible roostering?

You won't catch a Marxist driving a Jaguar.
NO, ARTHUR SCARGILL DRIVES TOO FAST!

I LOVE MY BL MAESTRO
— IT TOLD MY MOTHER-IN-LAW TO *◎✿❋ OFF!

I've bought head-rests for my car—Now I'm looking for mouth-rests for my wife and mother-in-law.

DO ARCHBISHOPS' CARS HAVE REV-COUNTERS?

I'VE GOT A TIGER IN MY TROUSERS

Lover of the Year 1931

watch my rear — not hers

PBC 172

I'M LOOKING FOR A RELIANT SEX-KITTEN

Little Bo-Peep come blow my horn.

PROFESSORS DO IT BY DEGREES.

Librarians make novel lovers.

SILENCE

PHOTOGRAPHERS DO IT IN THE DARK.

UNION LEADERS DO IT BY NEGOTIATION — AND STRIKE AFTERWARDS!

Bank managers do it with interest.

TOWN PLANNERS DO IT WITH THEIR EYES SHUT.

Book keepers do it with double entry.

CHARLES AND DI DO IT BY ROYAL APPOINTMENT.

Teachers do it with class.

TOMMY COOPER
DOES IT JUST LIKE THAT.

Gordon does it
in a Flash.

Morticians are
dead keen on it.

George
does
it
Best.

Morecambe
does it Wisely.

Paris does it plastered.

CYRIL SMITH DOES IT WITH SOME DIFFICULTY.

Lord Snowdon does it in soft focus.

BARRISTERS DO IT IN THEIR BRIEFS

Paul Daniels likes it —NOT A LOT

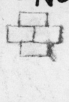

Rugby players do it with odd-shaped balls

SCRABBLE PLAYERS LAY SEVEN IN A ROW — —AND SCORE!

WANT ONE

Tennis players do it with new balls – and love all!

CONSERVATIONISTS DO IT NATURALLY.

MARATHON RUNNERS
KEEP IT UP FOR HOURS.

Piggott does it on the flat.

CHEFS MAKE A MEAL OF IT.

But too many cooks spoil the brothel.

CHINESE FOOD LOVERS WANT TO DO IT AGAIN AFTER 20 MINUTES —And the waiters watch!

WHEN IT COMES TO STUFFING
YOU CAN'T BEAT A TAXIDERMIST.
— or Paxo!

stewardesses
do it in the sky.

BARTENDERS DO IT
ON THE ROCKS.

Waitresses
serve it
on a tray.

Politicians
just talk
about it.

Musicians do it by the score.

THE TREORCHY
MALE VOICE CHOIR
DO IT ALL THROUGH THE NIGHT

Promenaders do it standing.

MONKS DO IT FROM HABIT.

NUNS WERE ONCE NOVICES AT IT.

And lay preachers believe in free love

RACING DRIVERS DO IT FROM POLE POSITION.

HIGHLAND DANCERS DO IT ON THEIR TOES.

SOLOMON GRUNDY,
☆◉◎◉✳✳◎ ON MONDAY
☆◉◎◉✳✳◎ ON TUESDAY,
☆◉◎◉✳✳◎ ON WEDNESDAY
☆◉◎◉✳✳◎ ON THURSDAY,
☆◉◎◉✳✳◎ ON FRIDAY
DIES ON SATURDAY,
BURIED ON SUNDAY
THIS IS THE END
OF SOLOMON GRUNDY.